Let's have an Art Attack!

WELCOME TO THE ART ATTACK ANN[UAL]
IT'S JAM PACKED WITH THINGS TO M[AKE] AND DO,
BURSTING WITH HINTS AND TIPS AND
OVERFLOWING WITH BRILLIANT THINGS TO KEEP
YOU BUSY FOR MONTHS!

WHETHER YOU'RE IN THE MOOD FOR DRAWING,
COLOURING, PAINTING OR PAPIER MACHÉ, I'VE
GOT IT COVERED!

REMEMBER YOU DON'T HAVE TO BE A GREAT
ARTIST TO HAVE FUN!

USEFUL STUFF!

old newspapers
cardboard box card
paper fasteners
mixing bowl
colouring pens
pencils
sticky tape
PVA glue
balloons
scissors
kitchen roll
toilet rolls
brushes
paints

£6.99

21 Greek Urn

**24** Colour By Numbers!

26 Monstrous Make

40 Secret Sheep

44 Treasure Chest

64 What a Hoot

shopping list
butter
milk
yoghurt
cheese
and
moo-oo-sli!

66 Animal Crackers

80 Out of this World

25
5   8
10
5
2

84 Shell Shocker

104 Money Box Mushroom

106 Choc-a-doodle-do

PAPIER MACHE T

MODEL MAD!

1 Use sticky tape to join things together. Remember to use plenty of tape to make it really secure.

2 Then pad your shape out with newspaper, either crumpled or rolled and stick in place with more sticky tape.

3 Mix PVA glue and water together. For most models, 1 part PVA glue and 1 part water is about right. Slosh this all over and cover your make with strips of torn newspaper or kitchen towel.

4 Papier maché must be left to dry until it's rock hard. This can take from 8 hours up to 3 days depending on how thick the layers of paper are and what the weather's like! Then you can paint.

Tips!

Make sure you use plenty of diluted PVA so it soaks right into the paper.

Models built on a solid base of cardboard or plastic need about three to four layers of paper while papier maché shells made on balloons need at least 8 layers of paper.

To help you see where you have started another layer, use alternate layers of newspaper and magazine paper.

Use a paintbrush to push the soggy paper into all the cracks and crevices.

TIPS!

The great thing about papier mâché is that you can make loads of models out of rubbish! Remember to save boxes and packaging – you can make all sorts of things! Before you get started take a look at these hints and tips on making and painting papier mâché models.

PERFECT PAINT JOB!

Make sure the papier mâché is completely dry before painting, or the paint might crack or flake off.

First paint the whole model with white poster paint. This will give it a brighter finish and the newspaper print won't show through.

Now paint over the white paint using poster paints or acrylics. Leave squares of white for windows and doors.

When the paint has dried, use a black marker pen to add details like the bricks and windows on this model.

For a nice shiny finish, cover the whole thing with a coat of PVA glue. This will also help to stop the paint coming off.

If you want to paint it a different colour, begin again with a coat of white paint.

Paint can make such a difference! Take one basic model and paint it four different ways, to make a lighthouse, an ice cream, a comical road cone and a witch's hat!

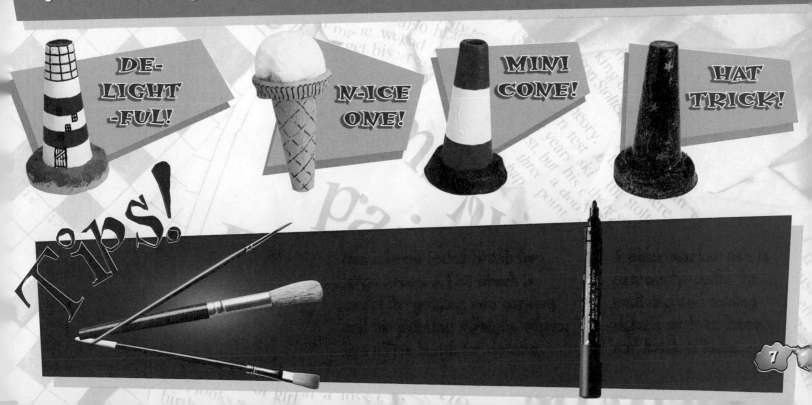

DE-LIGHT-FUL!

N-ICE ONE!

MINI CONE!

HAT TRICK!

Tips!

SNAIL MAIL!

THIS SNAIL'S SHELL MAKES A GREAT HOME FOR YOUR WRITING SETS. LETTERS AND IMPORTANT REMINDERS!

YOU WILL NEED:
Cardboard, scissors, sticky tape, newspaper, PVA glue, paints.

1 Draw a large snail shape like the one above on a piece of card. Cut it out. Then use it as a template to make a second one.

2 Cut a long strip of cereal box card about 6cm wide. (Stick several pieces together to make it longer.) Attach the snail cut outs to the middle of the strip taping them to the edges.

3 Tape the card strip along the back part of the snail shape stopping about half way up. Trim the strip. Do this to the front section as well - stopping before you reach the head.

4 Cut another strip the same width and tape it to the head section. Take your time, and you will get the card smooth and curved.

5 Roll 2 small tubes of card and tape them to the head. Make them wide enough to hold a pen in each. Stuff the inside of your snail with newspaper to keep it in shape.

6 Now cover the snail's body with 2 layers of torn newspaper pasted on with diluted PVA glue. Leave it to dry over night.

PVA

7 Lay the snail on one side to build up the 'shell.' Stick on sausage shapes of newspaper in a spiral shape. Leave to dry before turning it over and doing the other side.

PVA

8 When that's dry, cover the whole thing with another layer of papier maché. Use a brush to push the wet paper into all the crevices. Leave it to dry, then remove the newspaper stuffing.

9 Now you can paint your mail snail. When the paint has dried, put your envelopes and paper into his shell.

RATHER THAN GOING FOR 'SNAILY' COLOURS, WHY DON'T YOU PAINT YOUR SNAIL IN BRIGHT COLOURS TO MATCH YOUR ROOM?

NEIL'S GREAT ESCAPE!

NEIL'S IN A HURRY - HE'S GOT SOME ART ATTACKS TO DO AND HE NEEDS YOUR HELP! USE A PENCIL TO HELP HIM ESCAPE FROM THIS CRAZY MAZE!

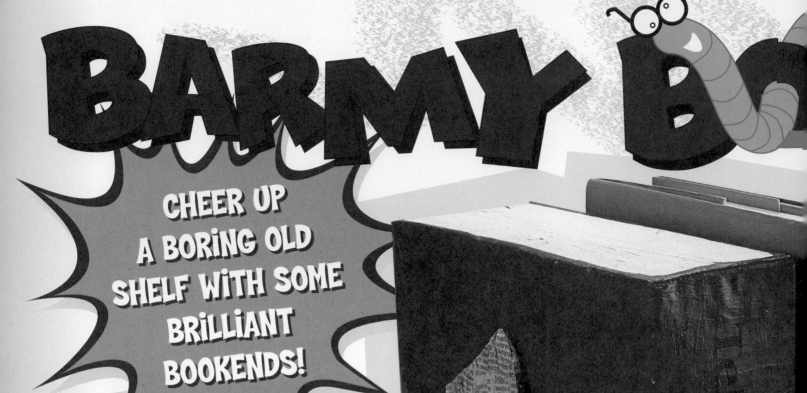

BARMY BO

CHEER UP A BORING OLD SHELF WITH SOME BRILLIANT BOOKENDS!

YOU WILL NEED:

2 cereal boxes, gravel or sand, sticky tape, cardboard, newspaper, 2 plastic carrier bags, string, PVA glue, paints.

1 Pour some sand or gravel into 2 cardboard cereal boxes the same size. Then stuff them with newspaper. Tape the boxes closed with sticky tape.

OKWORM!

WRITE FUNNY TITLES ON THE SIDES OF YOUR BOOKENDS. WHAT ABOUT 'THE CLIFF ACCIDENT' BY EILEEN DOVER OR 'BULL FIGHTING' BY MATT ADOR?

2 Stick a piece of thick card to the base of each box in an L shape and a backwards L shape. Use plenty of sticky tape to make it quite sturdy.

3 Cut a piece of card to fit the front of one of the boxes. Cut a hole in the centre and bend the pieces out to make it look like something has ripped through. Stick the piece of card to one of the boxes with sticky tape.

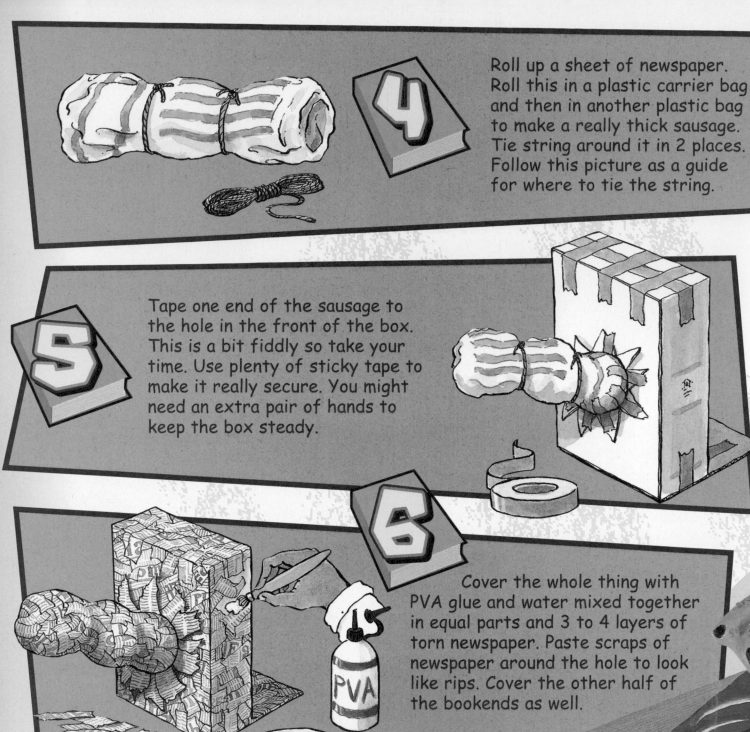

Roll up a sheet of newspaper. Roll this in a plastic carrier bag and then in another plastic bag to make a really thick sausage. Tie string around it in 2 places. Follow this picture as a guide for where to tie the string.

5 Tape one end of the sausage to the hole in the front of the box. This is a bit fiddly so take your time. Use plenty of sticky tape to make it really secure. You might need an extra pair of hands to keep the box steady.

6 Cover the whole thing with PVA glue and water mixed together in equal parts and 3 to 4 layers of torn newspaper. Paste scraps of newspaper around the hole to look like rips. Cover the other half of the bookends as well.

7 When it's dry, you can paint it. Don't paint the newspaper around the hole so that it looks like the worm has eaten through the book. Give him a funny face! Finally stick little pieces of newspaper in his mouth.

CROC ENDS!

USE YOUR IMAGINATION TO CREATE DIFFERENT KINDS OF BOOKENDS. SCRUNCH NEWSPAPER IN TO TRIANGULAR JAW SHAPES TO MAKE THE FACE OF A CROCODILE. ADD BALLS OF PAPER FOR EYES AND A CARDBOARD TONGUE. COVER WITH PAPIER MACHÉ AND PAINT.

HOT TIP!

If your bookends are not heavy enough they will topple over. Check before you cover with papier maché so you can open them up and fill them with some more sand!

ARTY ACT[

ROUND THE BEND!

SOLVE THE CROSSWORD BY READING THE CLUES. THE LAST LETTER OF EACH ANSWER IS THE FIRST LETTER OF THE NEXT ANSWER.

1. The opposite of dark.
2. Copying an image using transparent paper.
3. Mix blue and yellow to get this colour.
4. Use it for papier maching models.
5. Useful for drawing straight lines.
6. A bright, primary colour.
7. Another word for sketching.
8. Sticky substance used for joining things.
9. Removes unwanted pencil lines.
10. To reuse something again.

SPOT THE DIFFERENCE!

SEE IF YOU CAN SPOT THE SIX DIFFERENCES IN THE SECOND

16

VITIES!

DOUBLE TAKE!

I'VE TIDIED OUT ALL MY ART EQUIPMENT! LOOK AT BOTTOM BOX AND SEE IF YOU CAN SPOT WHICH 3 THINGS I'VE THROWN AWAY!

17

Answers: The sharpener, orange paint brush and blue paintbrush are missing.

HOW TO DRAW

Here are a few tips to give you a different view on things! Add humour to your cartoons by drawing some distorted images!

When you look through straight glass, the image is not distorted.

When you look into a rounded fish bowl a fish will look out of shape. The part of the fish that is closest to the glass looks larger.

The glass in a door's peep hole is curved. If you look through the hole, people look short and fat...

...this is because the more curved glass in the centre magnifies the person in the middle more than the less curved glass around the edge.

DISTORTED VIEWS!

ooo

Have a go at drawing a cartoon character with thick lens glasses on. The same thing will happen as the peep hole glass distortion. It can look quite comical!

Another great distortion effect is through cracked mirrors! Draw lots of jagged shapes on to a piece of paper. Now draw a face, giving it a 'broken' look in each jagged section.

An obvious one is to draw a magnifying glass! What would your writing look like through it? If you've got a magnifying glass, take a look and draw what you can see.

MAG NIFIED

TURN OVER THE PAGE TO HAVE A GO YOURSELF!

TRY IT YOURSELF!

Try drawing three distorted images below in the hall of mirrors.
Will the curved mirrors make them tall, thin, short or fat?

GREEK URN

HOW ABOUT MAKING AN AUTHENTIC-LOOKING ANCIENT GREEK VASE? WELL HERE'S HOW...

YOU WILL NEED!
Round balloon, corrugated card, cardboard, newspaper, sticky tape, PVA glue, paints.

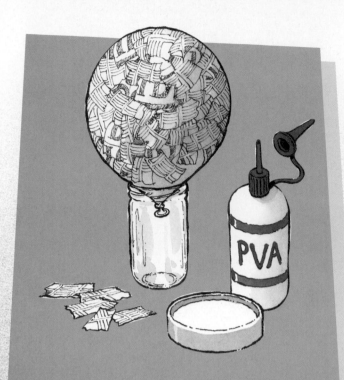

Blow up a round balloon and stick one end in a jam jar to balance it. Cover the balloon with diluted PVA glue and 3 layers of torn newspaper strips.

When dry, remove from the jam jar. Position the balloon so the larger end is at the top. Cut out 2 narrow card strips and attach them to the top and bottom of the balloon.

Now cut out 2 card handles and attach one to either side using masking tape. If they are too bendy, stick several pieces of card together to make them stronger.

Cut out 2 circles of card the same size but bigger than the bottom of the urn. Stick the circles together and then tape to the base.

Roll some narrow sausage shapes from dry newspaper and tape to the rim of the urn and the base circles. Follow this picture as a guide.

Cover the whole thing with 3 layers of newspaper strips and diluted PVA glue paying particular attention to the joins. Leave to dry until rock hard.

Carefully pierce the papier maché shell at the top of the balloon and the balloon will deflate. Remove any loose pieces.

Paint the urn as shown or decorate it as you wish. Look in books for Greek designs and copy one onto your 'Greek Urn.'

COLOUR BY N

UMBERS!

Use the colour guide to complete this picture that will leave you feline good!

4=RED

5=GREEN

6=BLUE

25

MONSTER

NEED SOMEONE TO HOLD YOUR BEDROOM DOOR OPEN? WHO BETTER THAN FRANKENSTEIN'S MONSTER?

YOU WILL NEED:

Plastic bottle, sand, newspaper, sticky tape, scrap card, PVA glue, paints, black marker pen.

HE'LL CERTAINLY SCARE AWAY ANY UNWANTED GUESTS...

1 Fill a clean plastic bottle with sand or small pebbles and put the lid back on, tightly. Cut out a feet shaped piece of card and tape it to the bottom with sticky tape.

2 Now twist newspaper into sausage shapes and attach to the sides of the bottle with sticky tape to form arms. Scrunch newspaper into balls to build up the feet.

3 Roll up newspaper for the head. Attach smaller rolls of paper for the eyebrows, mouth and nose. Attach the head on to the body. Cover with 5 layers of torn paper pasted on with PVA glue.

4 When completely dry and rock hard, you can paint. Finally, use black marker pen to add horrible looking scars!

MAKE ONE OF YOUR FAVOURITE CARTOON CHARACTERS OR SUPERHEROES INTO A DOORSTOP! FOLLOW THE STEPS FOR FRANKENSTEIN'S MONSTER BUT TAILOR THEM FOR YOUR OWN DESIGN. USE PICTURES TO HELP YOU BUILD UP THEIR FEATURES AND PAINT THEM CORRECTLY.

1 Start by making a box! Cut five squares of thick cardboard measuring 16cm x 16cm. Secure them together with plenty of sticky tape.

2 Blow up two balloons, one slightly bigger than the other. Make a small hole in the top of the box, place a cardboard ring from a roll of sticky tape on the box, then push the knot of the larger balloon through the hole and tape to the inside of the box.

3 Now take plenty of sticky tape and wind it around the knot on the other balloon. Then stick this balloon on top of the first one to make the head.

28

OLDER!

YOU WILL NEED:

scrap card, balloon, newspaper, sticky tape reel, straws, paints, PVA glue, sticky tape.

DO YOU WANT A HOLDER THAT IS OUT OF THIS WORLD, WELL WHAT YOU NEED IS AN ALIEN CD HOLDER...

For the legs and the antennae, make little snips in the ends of eight bendy drinking straws, and tape in place on the body and head.

5

Cover the whole thing, inside and out, with torn newspaper pasted on with diluted PVA glue. (7 to 8 layers on the balloons and 2 to 3 layers on the box.) For the legs and antennae, you may find it easier to use kitchen roll.

6

Once your CD rack is completely dry, paint it and give him a face. Add some glitter for a that final galactical feel!

PAINTING AN ALIEN FACE GIVES YOU A GREAT OPPORTUNITY TO BE CREATIVE! HERE ARE SOME IDEAS FOR SOME DIFFERENT FACIAL EXPRESSIONS.....

SCARY ALIEN!

SILLY ALIEN!

HAPPY ALIEN!

THE BOX IS THE RIGHT SIZE TO HOLD CD ROMS OR CDS UPRIGHT OR HORIZONTALLY.

MAKE IT A BIT BIGGER TO HOLD BOOKS, IF YOU LIKE.

30

GIANT WORDSEARCH!

```
N T R A C I N G B E V Q C Y R
E N E K A R E N O R A N G E T
W A T E R C O L O U R S F L N
S R T J F A R I S Y N T N L A
P A I N T R K A X P I R I O L
A E L E I D S R Y U S A T W W
P K G H A B F T G O H W K H A
E A O R N O S O V N N S B C T
R K P E L A O R C F I S L T E
K C E E U R U L E R E R V E R
D R N K R D E N B D X W T K V
G A C P J L S C I S S O R S P
L K I T C H E N R O L L Q V U
U D L G L D Q I H P A S T E L
E B O K N R U B B E R K A Y P
S N L W S T I C K Y T A P E A
U B R U S H N F E L T T I P S
M A R K E R S O A N T I N R O
D A Z R B X P B H D U N K L U
```

PAINT	PENCIL	PINK	MARKERS	KITCHEN ROLL	SKETCH
BLUE	GREEN	STRING	SEQUINS	WATERCOLOUR	PULP
GLUE	SCISSORS	STICKY TAPE	GLITTER	NEWSPAPER	WATER
PAPER	ORANGE	TRACING	ART	CARDBOARD	BRUSH
YELLOW	RUBBER	CRAYON	VARNISH	STRAWS	PASTEL
RED	RULER	FELT TIPS			

Neil's Quick Draw Tour!

I'M OFF ON HOLIDAY – WHY DON'T YOU HELP ME PACK MY BAGS AND JET OFF? COMPLETE THE PICTURES BY COPYING THE IMAGES IN THE MARGIN. THEN FINISH AND COLOUR ALL THE POSTCARDS FROM THE PLACES I'VE BEEN.

I'm packing for a mystery whirlwind holiday! What are the last few items I need to pack?

At the Airport!

DEPARTURES GATES 1-4

COME ON! THE SOONER YOU DRAW MY PLANE, THE SOONER I'LL FIND OUT WHERE I'M GOING!

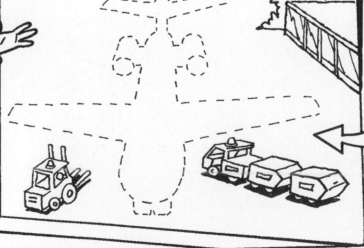

Draw these things in the space!

Copy this plane over the dotted lines.

And finally, taking the plunge in Greece!

But the best part of any trip is coming home to the things you love! Like Art Attack!

No sharks please!

AH.... HOME SWEET HOME!

35

SUPER SCRIBBLERS!

Write it all down with these great pens. You can make any kind of super scribbler you want. Here are a few ideas!

1 Draw a circle on some thin card. Divide it into quarters and cut them out. Roll one of the quarters into a cone shape around a pen. Snip the narrower end off. Make sure the end of the pen sticks out.

2 Secure the cardboard cone with sticky tape. Put some tape around the narrow end of the cone to hold the pen in place. Stick the other end down as well.

DYNAMITE

EXPLOSIVE IDEA!

Start with a rectangle of card. Roll it around your pen quite loosely and stick together with sticky tape. Stuff the gap around the pen with kitchen roll. Make sure the end of the pen is sticking out. Tape a short piece of string to the other end. Papier mache the whole thing with 2 layers of kitchen roll and let dry. Then paint like dynamite!

TASTY TREAT!

Follow steps 1 to 3. Then wrap a rectangle of card around the wider end and stick down to form the cone. Make sure this sticks up slightly so you can stick a scrunched up ball of newspaper in the middle to make 'ice-cream.' Cover with 2 layers of papier maché and let dry. Paint like an ice-cream. I added some small beads with PVA glue on top!

3 Cover the cardboard cone with 2/3 layers of papier maché. Make sure you put some on the join between the cardboard and the pen nib. Leave to dry until rock hard.

4 Now decorate. If you want to make it into a carrot, paint it orange. Add shredded tissue paper to the top to look like a real carrot!

CAN YOU THINK OF SOME OTHER SUPER SCRIBBLERS TO MAKE? WHAT ABOUT A BANANA, A FLOWER OR A CATERPILLAR?

SUPER SCRIBBLERS

TRACE iT!

Blast into space with this wicked trace it! Simply trace the pictures from the left hand page onto the right hand panel to create your own alien world!

SECRET SH

1 Attach four toilet rolls to the bottom of an empty shoebox with sticky tape. These are the legs.

2 Wrap a layer of corrugated card around the end of each toilet roll to make hooves.

3 Cover the shoebox and four legs with two layers of torn newspaper pasted on with diluted PVA glue. Leave to dry.

4 Turn the box the correct way up and replace the lid. Scrunch up balls of newspaper and tape them on to build up the body. Leave a space for the head.

EEP!

EWE'D BE BA..A..RMY NOT TO MAKE THIS! TRANSFORM AN OLD SHOEBOX INTO A FANTASTIC SHEEP! NOT ONLY DOES IT LOOK SHEEP-TASTIC IT HIDES ALL YOUR SECRET STUFF TOO!

YOU WILL NEED:

Shoebox with lid, corrugated card, 4 toilet rolls, sticky tape, newspaper, PVA glue, paints, green paper.

5

Cover the whole thing with two layers of papier maché, but do not join the lid to the base. Use large pieces of paper to cover the balls of paper. Leave to dry with the lid off.

PVA

41

6 Make the sheep's head by rolling a large piece of corrugated card into a tube shape. Stuff it with newspaper. Cut out card ears and tape them on either side.

7 Tape the head to the body and cover with two layers of papier maché, paying particular attention to the joins. Leave to dry.

8 Now decorate! Paint the fleece white and the head and legs black. Paint some eyes on his face. Finally cut out a piece of grass from green paper or card and stick it to his mouth.

PVA

USE YOUR SHEEP AS A SECRET HIDEAWAY! HIDE YOUR DIARY OR ANYTHING ELSE FROM PRYING EYES!

HOT TIP! Add grey highlights to the sheep's body to give it a more textured effect!

SNACK ATTACK!

CREATE SOME MINI MODEL FOOD FOR AN ART ATTACK PICNIC!

Salt dough recipe!

PLAIN FLOUR, SALT , WATER, VEGETABLE OIL.

1. Mix together equal amounts of the flour and salt.
2. Add a little oil and enough water to make a dough.
3. Use your hands to knead the mixture into a soft dough ball.
4. Use the dough straight away to make models or store it, wrapped in cling film, in the fridge, for up to three days.
5. Leave your models to harden for a couple of days before painting them.

CLEANING DIRECTIONS

Allow dough to dry then loosen it with a brush and vacuum. If necessary, rinse with gentle soap, cold water and a brush.

START!

1 Break off pieces of dough, roll it into balls to create oranges and tomatoes. Roll it into long sausage shapes to make a cucumber or bananas. Squash both ends flat to make a drinks can.

2 Roll a larger piece into a ball and then flatten it on either side to make a cake. Carefully cut a slice out of the cake to make it look real. Flatten a ball of dough to make a pizza.

3 You can copy the other things in the picture or create some of your own favourite food.

4 When you have moulded your shapes, simply leave to dry overnight before painting.

5 Finally use a scrap piece of fabric or a hanky to make a picnic rug.

EVEN IF YOU'RE NOT A PIRATE YOU'LL BE TEMPTED BY THIS TREASURE CHEST! FOLLOW THE SIMPLE STEPS TO MAKE A COOL CHEST TO STORE YOUR MONEY OR SECRET STUFF!

1 Cut out 5 rectangles of card, two measuring 20.5cm x 10.5cm (front & back), two measuring 12.5cm x 10.5cm (sides) and one measuring 20.5cm x 12.5cm for the base. Stick them together with sticky tape.

2 Cut 4 strips of card, two measuring 20.5cm x 2.5cm and two more measuring 12.5cm x 2.5cm. Stick these inside the top of the box, so they stick up slightly.

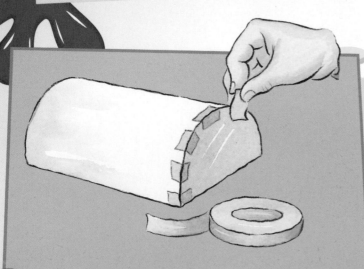

3 For the lid, cut a rectangle measuring 21.5cm x 20.5cm. Now cut a circle in half to make two equal semi circles. Curve the rectangle around the half circles and join together with sticky tape.

4 Cut a keyhole shape from scrap card and stick it to the front of the box. Stick a length of string around the keyhole, in a swirly pattern.

PVA

YOU WILL NEED
Scrap card, string, newspaper, paints, PVA glue, sticky tape.

5 Cover the box with two layers of torn newspaper pasted on with diluted PVA glue. When it's dry, paint. Make it look wooden by using brown and yellow paint.

IT DOESN'T HAVE TO BE A 'WOODEN' CHEST. PAINT IT ANY COLOUR YOU LIKE. IT WILL LOOK GREAT IN ANY ROOM.

WHAT ABOUT MAKING A KEY TO GO WITH YOUR TREASURE CHEST?

SIMPLY CUT OUT A KEY SHAPE FROM CARDBOARD. PAD IT OUT WITH NEWSPAPER AND THEN COVER WITH PVA GLUE MIXED IN EQUAL AMOUNTS WITH WATER AND 2 LAYERS OF KITCHEN ROLL. WHEN IT'S DRY. PAINT.

HOW TO DRAW

Blow your mind with these ear bashing sound effects. Here's some great ideas for making your pictures and cartoons really LOUD!

Draw words or noises coming from animals or people. I've drawn a dog and then, with a pencil, I marked two lines coming from its mouth in a cone shape. In between the lines I wrote 'gggrr,' stretching the word to add emphasis.

Robots make lots of noises. Think of a robot noise and write it down so that you know how it looks, think about where it comes from, then draw it in.

Water dripping sounds sloppy, make your words look like they are made of water. When a tap drips it makes the same sound over and over, so repeat the words in your drawing.

A bee leaves its buzz behind. I've drawn a buzzing trail behind my bee to show both the noise it makes and the direction it has flown in.

46

oooo SOUND EFFECTS!

Rockets zoom off into space. This drawing really gives you a feeling off blasting off!

ZOOM!

If someone was snoring, the noise they made would be jagged and vibrating to give an impression of thunderous snoring.

SNORE

You can use the size of your letters to indicate the volume of your sound effect. I've made the 'shh' letters small to show that the noise is quiet and then made them larger to make the sound louder and louder.

SHHH

SHHHHH

SHHHHHHH

BRRR

When it's cold you shiver, so write the word around your character making it look shivery by adding wiggly lines. The edges of the letters drip down to give it a wet and icy feeling.

TURN OVER THE PAGE TO HAVE A GO YOURSELF!

TRY IT YOURSELF!

Use this picture to practice drawing sound effects. Fill all the white space around the drawing with sound effects.

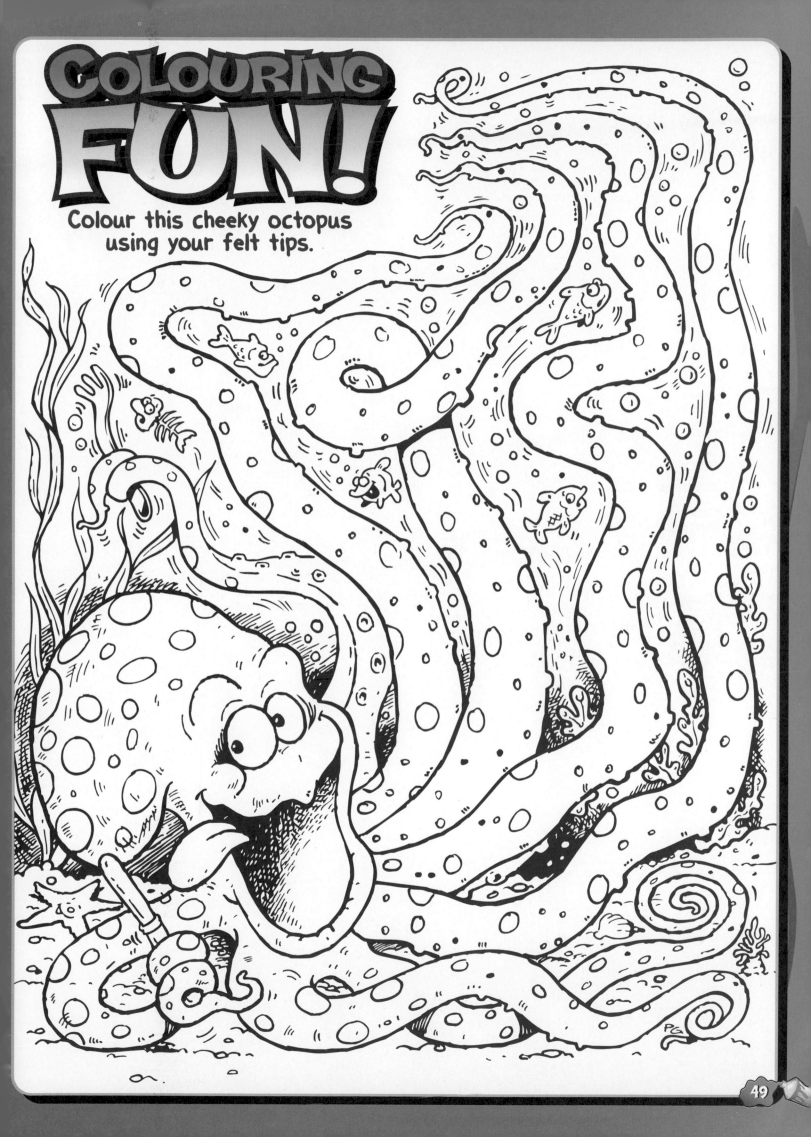

COLOURING FUN!

Colour this cheeky octopus using your felt tips.

WACKY WARMER

YOU WILL NEED:
Plasticine, plastic carton, newspaper, PVA glue, sticky tape, straws, scrap card, kitchen roll, paints.

CRACK ON FOR A REALLY SMASHING ART ATTACK! FOLLOW THE EASY STEPS BELOW TO CREATE THIS EGG-TASTIC EGG CUP!

You'll need a suitably shaped mould such as a very small balloon or make a mould from modelling clay. Cover the mould with cling film. Slosh on diluted PVA and cover with at least 5 layers of torn newspaper. Leave to dry.

Meanwhile make the base. Cut a length of toilet roll tube the same height as your plastic carton. Place it in the centre and tape in place. Stuff the gaps around the toilet roll tube with kitchen roll.

Papier maché the whole base including the gap between the edge of the carton and the toilet roll to make a flat surface.

When the egg 'shell' is dry, remove the mould. If it's a balloon, pop it and remove the pieces. Trim the edges so that the shell will sit comfortably on the base.

Cut bendy straws into arms and legs. Cut slits in one end of each straw and attach to the shell. Tape cardboard hands to the arms and feet shapes to the legs. Now cover the whole thing with a layer of papier maché and leave to dry.

STICK THESE HILARIOUS PICTURES ON TO YOUR EGGS WITH A SPOT OF GLUE!

AND FINALLY....

DECORATE THE WHOLE THING! PAINT CLOTHES AND A JOLLY FACE ON THE EGG. ADD DETAILS IN BLACK MARKER PEN. PAINT THE BASE TO LOOK LIKE A BRICK WALL.

YOU WILL NEED: Cardboard box card, string, PVA glue, sand, black marker pen, poster paints.

1 Take a large piece of thick card - the side piece from a cardboard box. Draw a simple picture and a border or frame. Use this picture as a guide.

STUFF!

Squirt or brush PVA glue onto the lines only and press on lengths of string. Leave to dry.

3 Slop loads of PVA glue onto the whole of your picture. Then sprinkle sand onto everything. Let the sand sink into the glue, and shake off the excess. Leave until it's completely dry.

4 Now paint your sand picture with bright poster paints. Use an old paint brush as the sand is quite rough. Paint the stringy bits black. (You could use a black felt tip pen.)

MAKE DIFFERENT SHAPED SAND PICTURES. KEEP THE PICTURES QUITE SIMPLE TO GET THE BEST RESULTS!

Secret Scrapbook

Keep a secret scrapbook! You'll find lots of pages to cut out and stick in your scrapbook over the next few pages. Write down things that you want to remember, stick in photos, sketch the people you meet and make silly checklists!

WHAT TO DO:

1 Cut out two pieces of thick card (109mm x 150mm)

2 Punch two holes in the sides for string or ribbon.

3 Pull out the centre pages (p56-57). Cut the pages up along the dotted lines and punch holes in the same place along the sides.

4 Thread string or ribbon through the back card, thread all the pages on and then thread the cover on.

5 Finally decorate the cover with your own design.

SEASIDE DIARY!

I made this look really beachy by adding shells. Find shells which already have holes in so you can attach them with string. I cut out seaside pictures and stuck them on the front with paper glue.

HANDS OFF - SECRET!

Create a scary cover to warn nosey parkers away! This one has been made with black card and white paint. I've even attached a small stick along the side by using string to tie the pages in and hold the stick on. It actually looks like a scary pirate's flag!

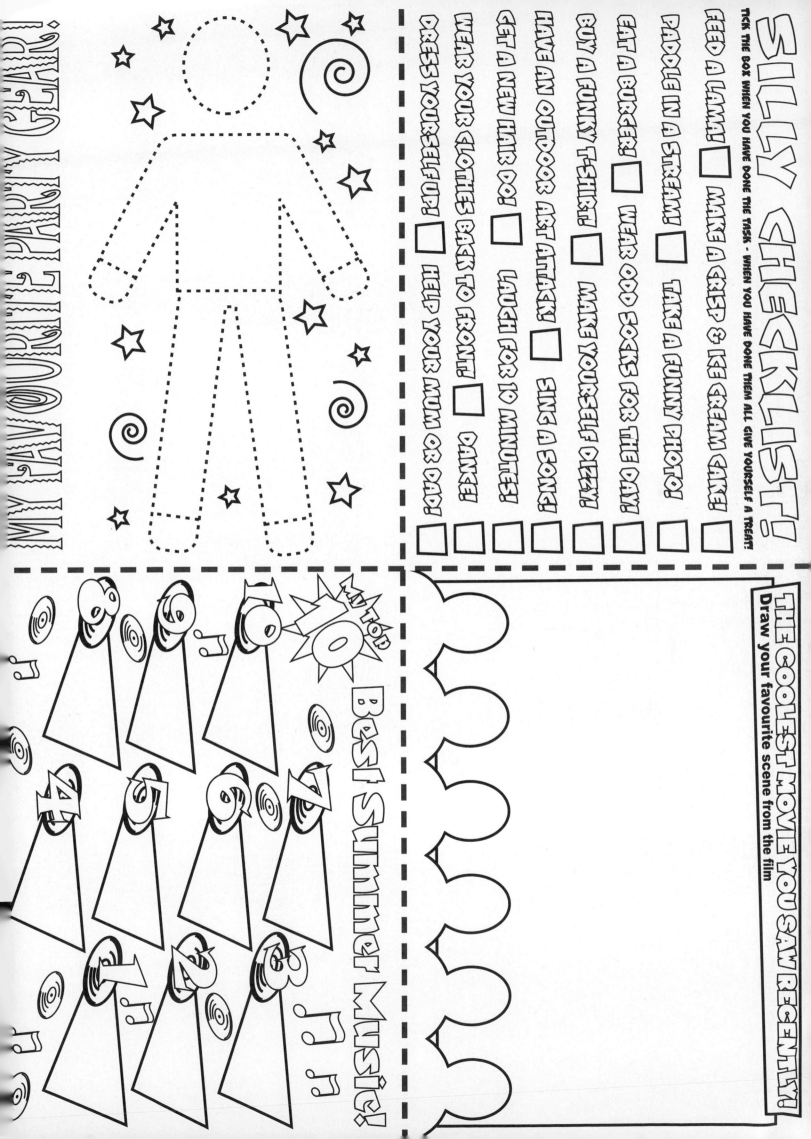

SILLY CHECKLIST!

TICK THE BOX WHEN YOU HAVE DONE THE TASK - WHEN YOU HAVE DONE THEM ALL GIVE YOURSELF A TREAT!

- FEED A LAMA! ☐
- MAKE A CRISP & ICE CREAM CAKE! ☐
- PADDLE IN A STREAM! ☐
- TAKE A FUNNY PHOTO! ☐
- EAT A BURGER! ☐
- WEAR ODD SOCKS FOR THE DAY! ☐
- BUY A FUNKY T-SHIRT! ☐
- MAKE YOURSELF DIZZY! ☐
- HAVE AN OUTDOOR ART ATTACK! ☐
- SING A SONG! ☐
- GET A NEW HAIR DO! ☐
- LAUGH FOR 10 MINUTES! ☐
- WEAR YOUR CLOTHES BACK TO FRONT! ☐
- DANCE! ☐
- DRESS YOURSELF UP! ☐
- HELP YOUR MUM OR DAD! ☐

THE COOLEST MOVIE YOU SAW RECENTLY!

Draw your favourite scene from the film

MY FAVOURITE PARTY GEAR!

Best Summer Music!

GAME ON!

Draw pictures of your favourite computer games and put the HI SCORES in the boxes!

Hi Score

Hi Score

Hi Score

MY NEXT GAME!

Self Portrait

Top 5 Lessons! Top 3 Teachers!

2

3

1

5

4

3

2

1

MY MINI COLLAGE!

MAKE A COLLAGE WITH ITEMS COLLECTED FROM YOUR TRAVELS.

Weather record

Day 1 ....
Day 2 ....
Day 3 ....
Day 4 ....
Day 5 ....
Day 6 ....
Day 7 ....
Day 8 ....
Day 9 ....
Day 10 ....
Day 11 ....
Day 12 ....
Day 13 ....
Day 14 ....

Sun
Clouds
Rain
Snow
Thunder
Wind
Fog

My name is ....
I live at ....
My hair is ....
I am ☐ years old
My best friend is ....
Birthday ....

Photo of me
Photo of me

AUTOGRAPHS!

DRAW PICTURES OF THE FRIENDS YOU MADE AND GET THEM TO SIGN THEIR NAMES!

My Favourite Meal!!

A scene from my holiday!

Draw a picture of a favourite scene, or stick in a photo or a postcard!

MY FAVOURITE POP STAR

...AD A £1,000,000 I WOULD BUY?

MUM

DAD

BRO/SIS

SIS/BRO

PET

ME

Stick it in the Bin!

This is the worst meal I ate!

QUICK ATTACK!

Use the colour guide to complete the picture and reveal what's hidden!

COLOUR CODE   ● =   — =   + =   X =

ANGRY KN

SEND A SHIVER DOWN THE SPINES OF VISITORS TO YOUR ROOM WITH A SUPER COOL BUT ANGRY KNOCKER! THESE GRUESOME GARGOYLES LOOK FANTASTIC AND THEY'RE PRETTY SCARY TOO!

OCKERS!

YOU WILL NEED:
Cardboard box card, scissors, sticky tape, sharp pencil, 2 small pebbles, PVA glue, newspaper, paints.

① Start by drawing an angry mouth on a piece of cardboard box card. Cut it out, draw around it on a second piece of card, then cut it out again - 2 pieces!

② Draw an ugly gargoyle face on a large piece of cardboard box and cut it out. There are 3 faces on this page to give you an idea!

③ Cut the face out. Tape one of the mouth pieces in place with sticky tape, then mark 4 dots - two above and two below the top lip, and stick the point of a sharp pencil through into sticky tack. Tape a pebble onto the bottom lip.

4 Build up the face using rolled up newspaper. Build up the lips and teeth within the mouth. Brush diluted PVA all over and cover with at least 2 layers of torn newspaper strips. Don't cover the pebble. Keep the holes above and below the mouth shape open.

5 To thicken up the knocker device (i.e. the second mouth shape), use twists of newspaper taped in place. Make it nicely rounded. Tape another small pebble in place. Cover with 2 layers of PVA and torn paper but do not cover the centre of the pebble.

6 Finally attach the second mouth shape to the top of the other one by tying it on with string. These are what the holes are for! Paint the knocker with black paint. Leave to dry then dab with gold or yellow paint.

ASK AN ADULT TO FIX IT TO YOUR BEDROOM DOOR. NOW MAKE SURE EVERYONE USES IT WHEN THEY COME TO DISTURB YOU!

ON THE OTHER HAND, YOU COULD MAKE A PRETTY KNOCKER! HERE'S AN IDEA FOR MAKING A FLOWERY ONE!

JUST IMITATE!

CREATE A PRICELESS MASTERPIECE WITH A FEW SNEAKY TIPS! IMPRESS EVERYONE WITH YOUR AUTHENTIC LOOKING OIL PAINTINGS...

All you need to create your cool painting is some card, tissue paper, PVA glue, water and poster paint.

IT LOOKS LIKE AN EXPENSIVE OIL PAINTING!

1 Use a piece of thick cardboard box card for the base of your painting.

2 Mix up some PVA glue and water in equal parts. Dip pieces of tissue paper or toilet roll in the mixture and place it on the cardboard base. Whatever you do, don't be neat. It needs to be lumpy!

3 When that has dried, sketch a still life using a pencil. I chose to draw a bowl of fruit!

4 Now paint the picture using poster paint keeping it nice and thick. Let it dry completely.

5 Finally brush your PVA mixture all over the painting so that it goes hard and shiny.

WHAT A HOOT!

YOU WON'T GET INTO A FLAP WITH THIS EASY MAKE! FOLLOW THE SIMPLE STEPS TO CREATE A FANTASTIC FLYING OWL!

1 Trace off the owl's body and wing template. Transfer to brown card and cut out two wings shapes and one body shape.

2 Trace off the face shape and transfer it to white card and cut out. This time make little snips all the way around the shapes to give an impression of feathers.

3 Trace the chest piece onto white or cream card and snip all the way around the edges to look feathery.

4 Glue the chest piece and two face shapes to the card, making sure the smaller face piece is on top. Now draw a face or cut out bits of paper and glue on for a face.

5 Make holes on the wings and body where shown. Fix the wings to the body using the paper fasteners.

6 Following the picture of the back of the owl as a guide, tie a short length of string to the other holes in the wings to make a loop. This allows you to make the wings flap.

ONCE YOU HAVE MADE THE OWL, HAVE A GO AT MAKING OTHER BIRDS OR ANIMALS. IF YOU WANT TO ADD LEGS, MAKE MORE HOLES IN THE BODY PART AND USE MORE PAPER FASTENERS.

ART ATTACK

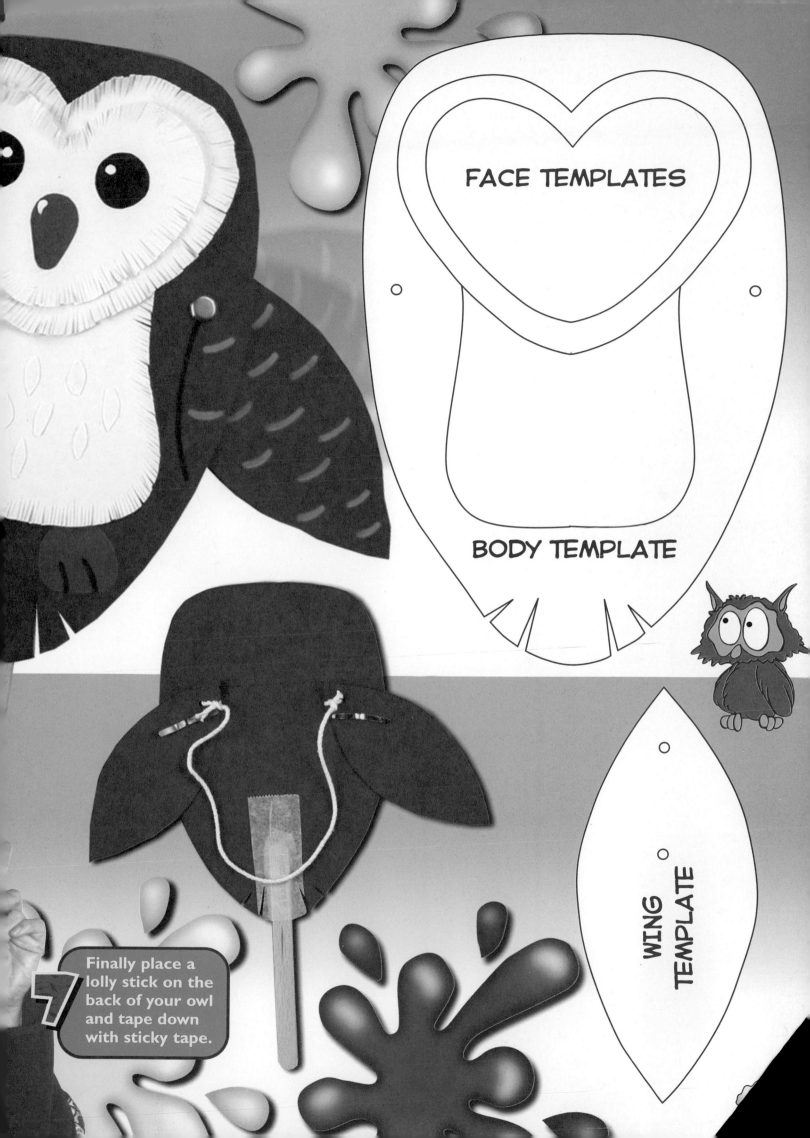

FACE TEMPLATES

BODY TEMPLATE

WING TEMPLATE

7 Finally place a lolly stick on the back of your owl and tape down with sticky tape.

ANIMAL CRA

GET READY FOR SOME REAL ANIMAL MAGIC! THESE FANTASTIC NOTEPADS ARE EASY TO MAKE AND THEY'D LIVEN UP ANY LIST!

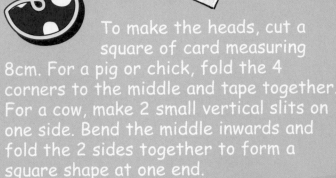

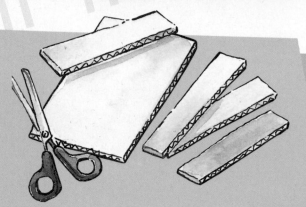

1 Cut a rectangle of thick card about 10cm x 14cm. Cut 4 strips of thinner card about 2cm x 7.5cm.

3 To make the heads, cut a square of card measuring 8cm. For a pig or chick, fold the 4 corners to the middle and tape together. For a cow, make 2 small vertical slits on one side. Bend the middle inwards and fold the 2 sides together to form a square shape at one end.

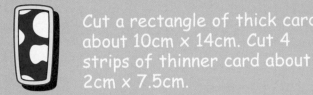

2 Roll the strips into little tubes. Tape them to the edges of the rectangle in these positions, making sure there is enough space for a pen or pencil.

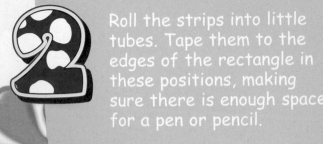

Oink! Oink!

shop

CKERS!

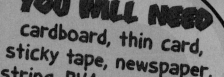

YOU WILL NEED cardboard, thin card, sticky tape, newspaper, string, PVA glue, paints, small notepads.

4 Tape the heads in place. Make ears and a tube like snout for the pig. Add ears to the cow and a beak to the chick. Attach a piece of string to the cow and pig for tails.

5 Cover them with 2 or 3 layers of torn newspaper and PVA glue mixed half with water. Cover the bottom of the pencil holders at the bottom of the notepad holder.

list

d'you feel like chicken... tonight?

6 Paint the notepad holders. When dry you can add any details with black marker pen. Attach a small notepad by gluing the back to the holder and add a couple of pens or pencils.

BABOUS

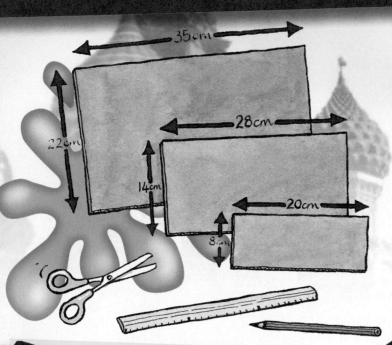

1 Cut out three rectangles of corrugated card to make the three bodies of the figures. Follow the measurements above.

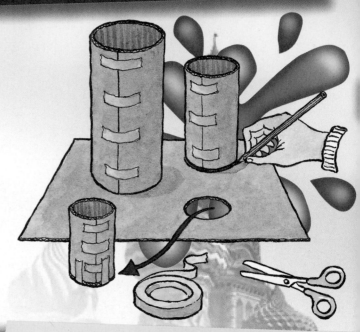

2 Roll up the pieces of card, to form cylinders, taping the short edges together. Place each one on a piece of thick card and draw around it. Cut out these three circles, and stick to one end of each cylinder to form a base.

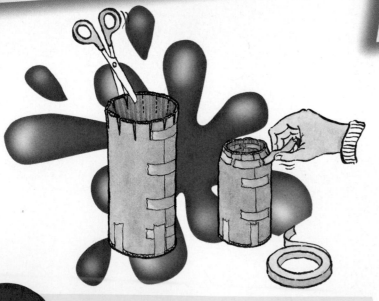

3 Snip into the top of each cylinder, to make small tabs. Press these inwards and tape in place with sticky tape.

4 Blow up 3 balloons for the heads. Tape them to the top of the bodies. (You can use crumpled balls of newspaper.)

5 Cover the shapes with three or four layers of papier mache on the bodies and seven or eight layers on the heads. Leave to dry until rock hard.

PVA

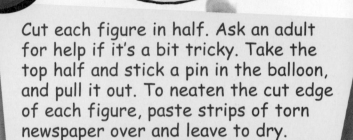

6 Cut each figure in half. Ask an adult for help if it's a bit tricky. Take the top half and stick a pin in the balloon, and pull it out. To neaten the cut edge of each figure, paste strips of torn newspaper over and leave to dry.

7 Cut three pieces of corrugated card, roll up, and slip inside the bottom half of each figure to make a 'lip'. Use the dimensions shown but you may need to adjust them depending on the thickness of your papier mache. Use glue to hold them in place.

31cm
24cm
18cm
14cm
8cm
7cm

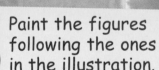

8 Paint the figures following the ones in the illustration.

HOT TIPS!

LEAVE THE TWO HALVES OF EACH DOLL SEPARATE WHILE THEY ARE DRYING OTHERWISE THEY WILL GET STUCK TOGETHER!

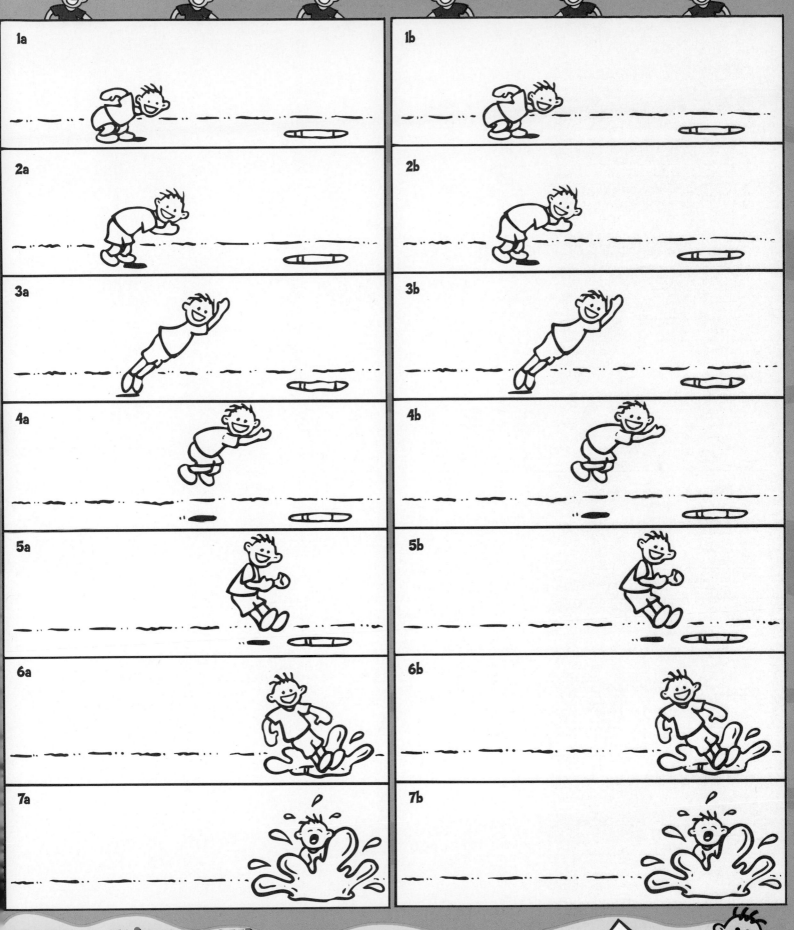

1a

1b

2a

2b

3a

3b

4a

4b

5a

5b

6a

6b

7a

7b

MAKE A FLICK BOOK!

Colour in the funny cartoon character above - remember he will be wearing the same thing in all the pictures. Stick the whole page onto card and then cut all the pictures out and place them in order - 1a, 1b, 2a, 2b and so on. Staple them together and then flick!

TRACE IT!

Run away and join the circus with this hilarious trace it! Simply trace the pictures from the left hand page onto the right hand panel.

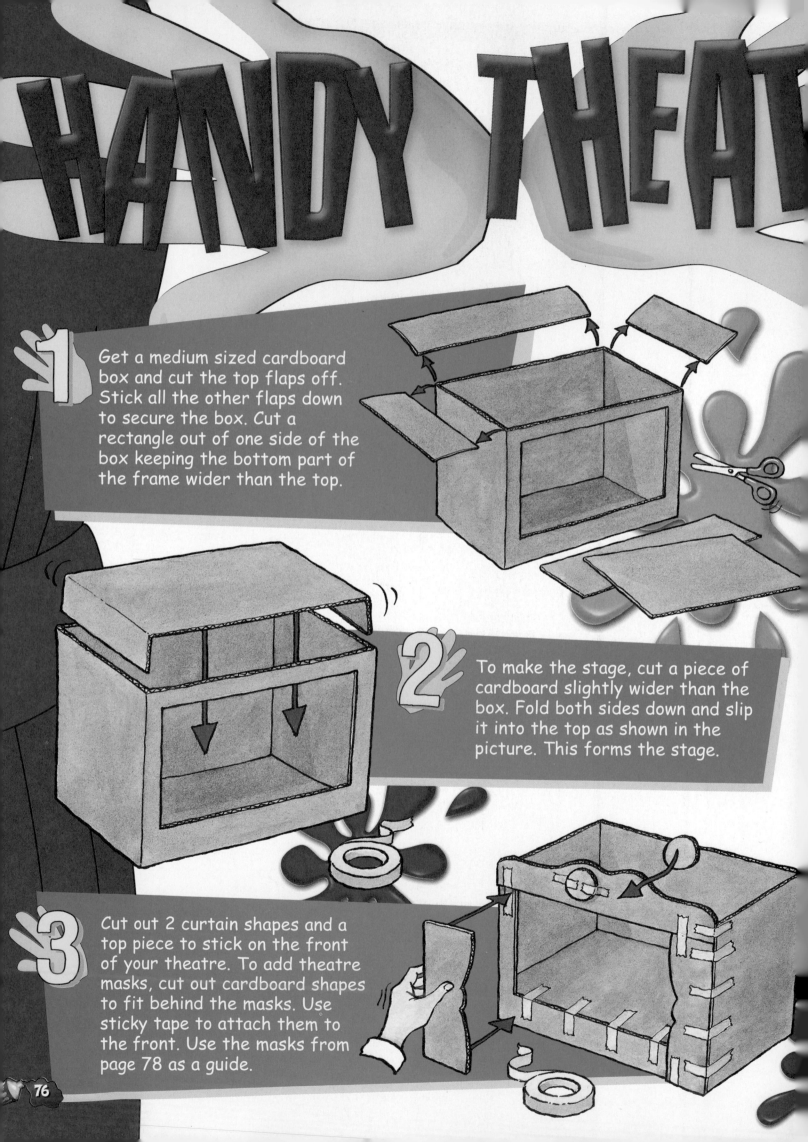

1 Get a medium sized cardboard box and cut the top flaps off. Stick all the other flaps down to secure the box. Cut a rectangle out of one side of the box keeping the bottom part of the frame wider than the top.

2 To make the stage, cut a piece of cardboard slightly wider than the box. Fold both sides down and slip it into the top as shown in the picture. This forms the stage.

3 Cut out 2 curtain shapes and a top piece to stick on the front of your theatre. To add theatre masks, cut out cardboard shapes to fit behind the masks. Use sticky tape to attach them to the front. Use the masks from page 78 as a guide.

4 Cut out 2 hand holes big enough for your hands to go through at the back. Now cover the whole thing with two layers of papier maché. Leave to dry.

PVA

5 Paint the whole thing white. When it has dried, decorate how you want. I have painted red curtains with gold trim and white masks. I painted the stage brown with black lines to look like planks of wood.

6 Paint a background scene on the back wall or draw it on to paper which you can slot in and out. Make sure you cut out holes for your hands in the correct places.

7 When it's dry, you can put black gloves on, grab some puppets and away you go! Take a look at page 79 for some puppet ideas!

THEATRE MASKS!

You can trace or copy these theatre masks to use. If they are the wrong size for your cardboard box, enlarge or reduce them on a photocopier. If you prefer just make up your own theatre masks. It's up to you!

TOY PUPPETS

What about using small toys to act out your favourite films or stories? The toys you can collect from fast food restaurants make great puppets!

FINGER PUPPETS

Finger puppets are easy to make. Just draw and cut out characters in card and make 2 holes at the bottom of them, large enough for you're fingers to go through.

SOCK PUPPETS

If you can't get hold of black gloves, why don't you make some sock puppets? Just add some button eyes and woolly hair.

79

OUT OF THIS

Shake your friends up with this great Art Attack! Capture your very own alien in a jar, surrounded by sparkling glitter just like stars!

1 Make sure that you've removed the labels from the jar and the lid. Cover the outside of the jar lid with PVA glue and place it in a saucer of glitter. Make sure that it is covered in glitter then leave it to dry.

2 When the lid is dry put some waterproof glue on the bottom of a lump of modelling clay and squash it down into the lid. Leave it to dry thoroughly.

3 Stick your alien model into the modelling clay with some more waterproof glue. Leave it to dry.

4 Fill the jar up with water. (You can use glycerine if you have it but be careful of your clothes and any furniture as it is very greasy.) Add some glitter.

WORLD!

YOU WILL NEED:

Jam jar with a lid, glue, glitter, water, modelling clay, small toy figure, (glycerine.)

TOP TIPS

n't use too much glycerine as the glitter ll not fall. You can use coloured glitter or d dye to make the scene different.

se a small toy from a keyring. What about trying a different shaped jar or some different toys for several glitter jars?

Screw the top of the jar on very tightly and then gently turn your shaker. Don't leave it on any furniture as the glycerine may stain.

81

$$ FUNNY MONEY! $$

Line your pockets with this funny money! You might not be able to spend it at the shops but you can have a laugh creating your own currency to swap with your friends!

WHAT TO DO:

1. Carefully remove these pages and stick them onto thin card or thick paper.

2. Photocopy them several times so you have lots of funny money!

3. Colour them in and then cut them out.

4. Add to your funny money by designing coins and other denominations. You could even stick on celebrity faces from magazines!

MUM DESERVES A REST! PAY HER 40 WINKS AND MAKE HER DAY!

N EXCHANGE FOR SOME MERITS, SEE IF YOUR BROTHER OR SISTER WILL HELP WITH YOUR HOMEWORK.

HAS SOMEONE DONE YOU A FAVOUR? GIVE THEM AN I.O.U WITH A CHOCOLATE NOTE!

83

SHELLISH

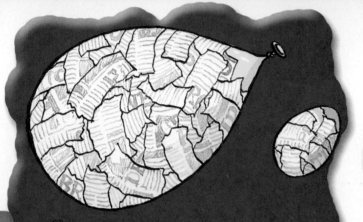

1 You can make this game any size you like. Use a balloon for a large game or an egg for a smaller game. Cover with three layers of papier maché.

2 When the egg shape is dry, remove the egg or burst the balloon. Trim the shell with scissors giving it a zigzag shape like a broken shell.

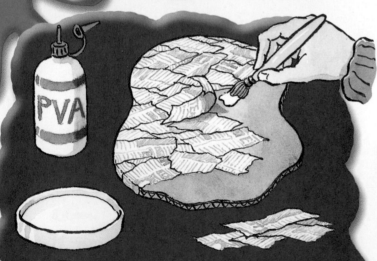

3 While that's drying, make the base. Cut a wobbly shape from thick cardboard. Cover the base with at least two layers of papier maché.

4 Stick the broken shell shape to the base with glue. Now paint. Leave it to dry then write numbers on with black marker pen. The highest number goes in the broken shell.

CKER!

THIS GAME CAN BE PLAYED BY YOURSELF OR WITH FRIENDS. THE AIM OF THE GAME IS TO FLICK YOUR TIDDLYWINKS OR COUNTERS ONTO THE HIGHEST NUMBERS. THE WINNER WILL BE THE ONE WITH THE HIGHEST SCORE AND NO MORE COUNTERS ON THE TABLE.

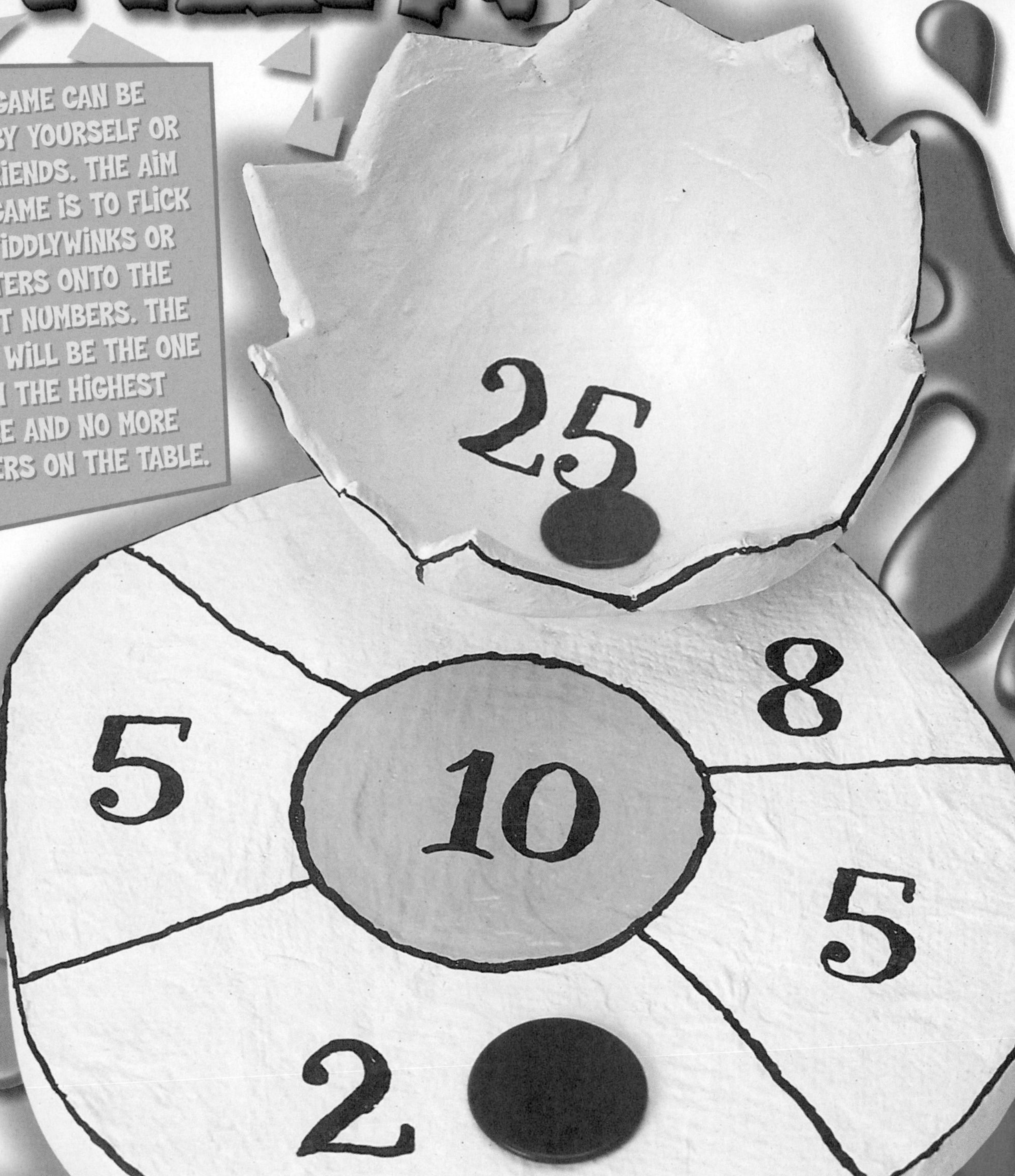

25

8

5

10

5

2

HOW TO DRAW

Drawing faces and heads at different angles can be quite tricky. Here's a step by step guide to help you stay ahead!

 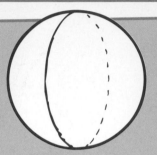 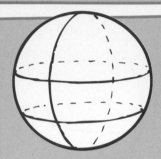

Start off with a circle for the head.

Divide the shape in two with a soft vertical guideline to indicate the tilt of the head.

Draw a soft horizontal guideline to indicate eye position and another at mouth position.

Try drawing guidelines on a ball or on an egg and view them from different positions.

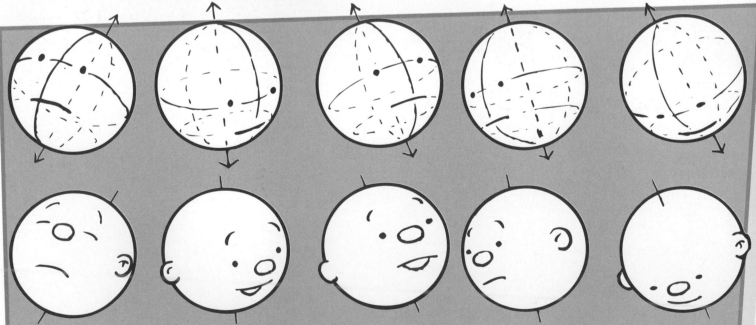

Use the guidelines to add the nose, mouth and eyes, copy the pictures to change the angle of the face. Keep the guidelines really soft so you can easily rub them out.

CARTOON HEADS!

Copy each stage of the pictures below then try to create some of your own. Start with the circle, add guidelines followed by eyes, nose and a mouth. Finally add ears, hair and any other features such as teeth, glasses or freckles.

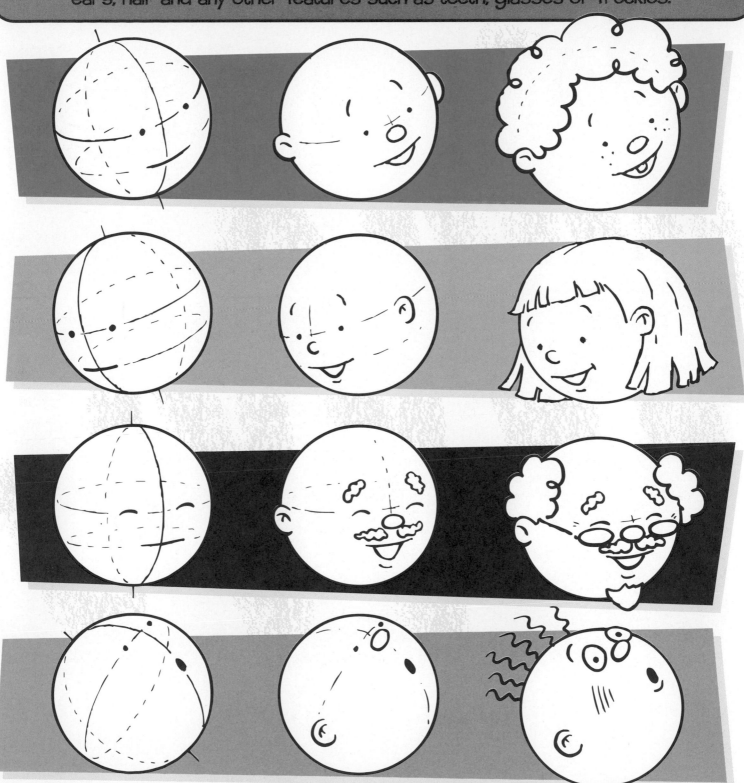

TURN OVER THE PAGE TO HAVE A GO YOURSELF!

TRY IT YOURSELF!

Now try drawing some heads on these headless characters
from the correct angle. Then try a few of your own!

MARVELLOUS MAPS!

OVER THE PAGE YOU'LL FIND YOUR MAP TEMPLATE. USE IT TO CREATE AN ANTIQUE MAP, A 3 DIMENSIONAL MAP OR A GAME!

ANTIQUE MAP!

1 Trace the map onto some plain paper. Paint all over the back with diluted PVA glue. This will make the paper stiffer and slightly transparent.

2 Fold and re-fold the map to make it as creased as possible.

3 Tear the edges of the map and rub them with brown crayon and then rub a damp tea bag over it to make it look old.

4 Give your map a title. Draw in mountains and trees and make up names for all the places on the island! Use old-fashioned writing!

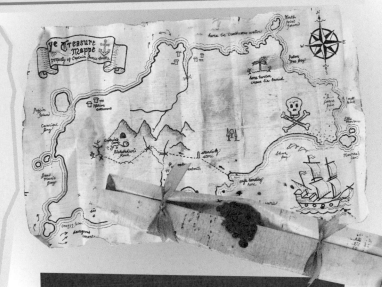

To make a seal, mix a drop of red paint with some PVA glue and blob it over the edge of the folded map. Press a chocolate coin wrapper into the centre to make a 'crest'.

3 DIMENSIONAL MAP!

1 Stick your map onto thick card. Slosh a layer of PVA glue over the whole thing.

2 Sprinkle some sand around the edges and build up the mountains with small bits of newspaper soaked in PVA glue.

3 Make little trees from dead matchsticks and balls of tissue.

4 Finally paint the map with poster paint.

X MARKS THE SPOT!

1 Stick the map onto plain paper. Colour it in using felt tips.

2 Write names all over the island.

3 Turn the map over and mark an x where the treasure is hidden!

4 Make little flags with everybody's names on them. Get some long pins and wrap a piece of paper round them and then glue down. (Ask an adult before handling pins.)

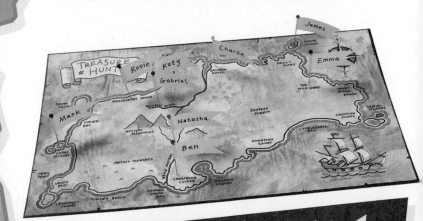

The winner is the person who places their pin nearest the treasure!

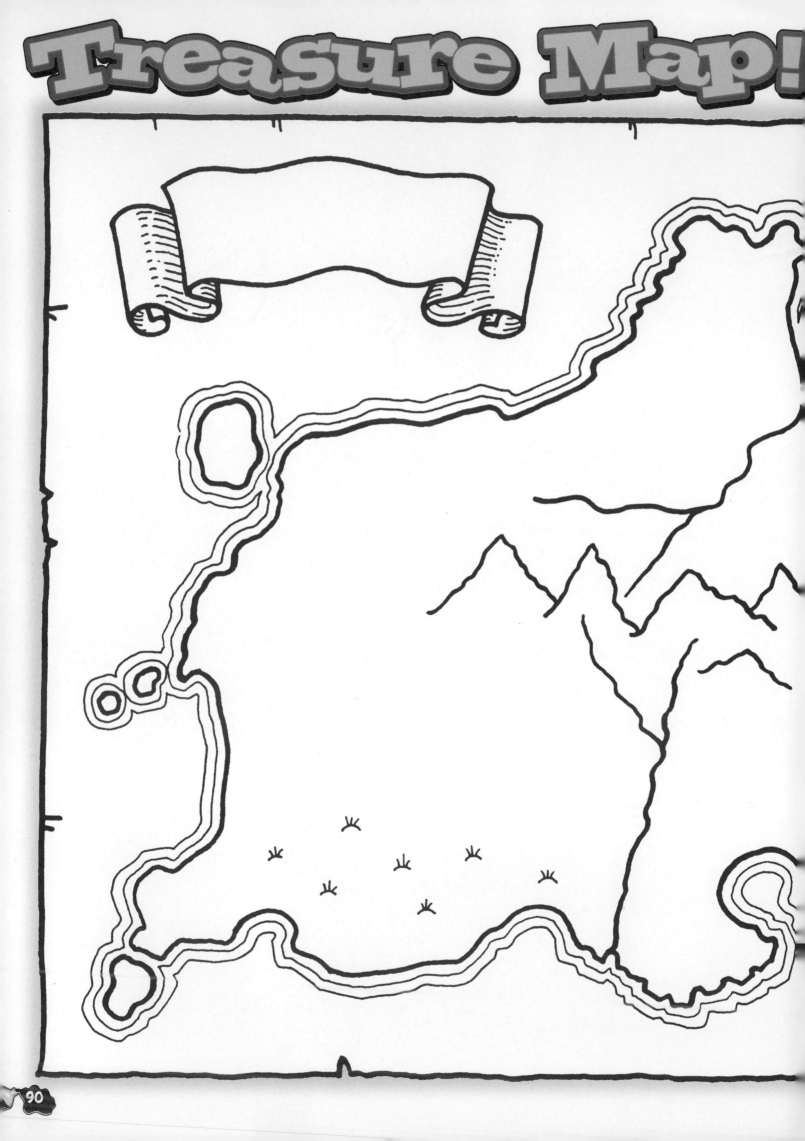

Here is your treasure map template. If you are going to make several different kinds of maps you will need to either photocopy these pages or trace the map on to plain paper.

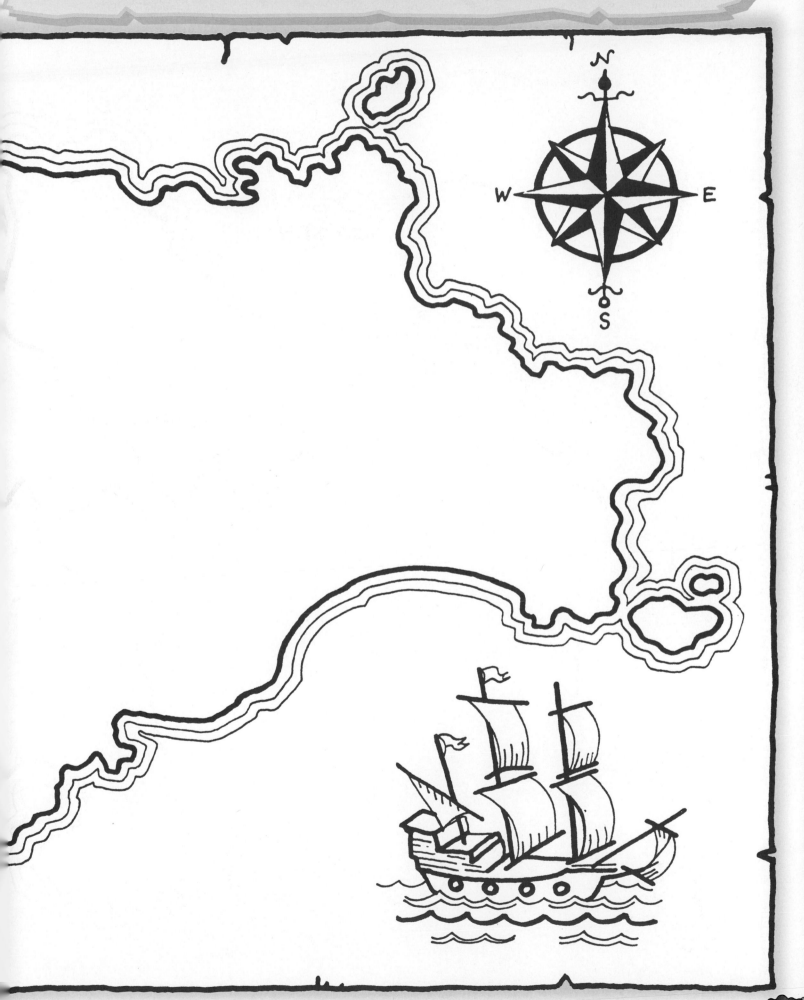

3-D JUGGLER!

CLOWN AROUND IN 3D WITH THIS OUTSTANDING IDEA! ONCE YOU KNOW HOW TO DO IT YOU CAN MAKE ALL SORTS OF PICTURES 3 DIMENSIONAL!

1 Carefully cut out picture 1 round its square border and stick it onto a piece of card. Colour it in. You could decorate the background too if you wish. This is the base of your 3D clown picture.

2 Cut out the clown from picture 2. This time cut away the T-shirt, leaving the braces and trousers. Colour it in the same colours as before. Stick small pieces of cardboard box card to the back of picture 2, then glue it down onto picture 1.

3 Colour in the juggling balls, hat, nose, hands and bowtie from picture 3 and then carefully cut them out. Stick little pieces of cardboard box card on the back of each item and glue them to picture 2..

HOLIDAY MADNESS!

HAVE A LOOK AT THE HILARIOUS SCENE BELOW. GUESS WHERE ALL THE ANIMALS HAVE BEEN ON HOLIDAY AND WRITE IT ON THEIR BAGS. THEN COLOUR IN YOUR PICTURE.

94

CRAZY COU

Scrunch tissue paper into balls and stick on to make leaves on the trees!

Cottonwool makes perfect clouds.

I created a little bird and added a real feather for a tail!

I've used a piece of blue wallpaper for the sky. It looks slightly textured.

Dead matchsticks make a great fence.

Use real twigs for branches

Cut down the side of a kitchen roll tube to make the trunks of the trees.

Cut out a very small section from the newspaper to create a mini newspaper!

Use green card, fabric or foam for the grass.

An old bit of material and some ribbon glued on makes a little bag.

Use fake or tissue flowers to add some colour.

Little beads glued on to the plates looks like rolls and grapes!

Cut out circles of card for picnic plates.

A small square of chequered fabric makes a cool tablecloth!

Create tiny sandwiches from small pieces of felt or cardboard.

96

AGES!

CREATE THESE COOL COLLAGES BY COLLECTING TEXTURED PAPER & CARD AND ANY SCRAPS OF RUBBISH YOU THINK WILL COME IN HANDY! USE PVA GLUE FOR ANY HEAVY MATERIALS AND A GLUE STICK FOR THINNER CARD AND PAPER. NOW GET STICKING!

Wispy clouds can be made from cottonwool.

Make larger clouds from felt, fabric or wadding.

This sun has been made from a lid covered in shiny foil. I added a smiley paper face!

Find something blue for the sky and sea. This is felt. If you build up layers you can get a wave effect.

More corrugated paper creates a super sandcastle.

Corrugated paper makes a wooden looking boat. The sails are simple white fabric.

Add real shells collected from any beach.

Make a mini newspaper from cut up newspaper. Just staple bits together.

How about a crab from folded paper - almost origami!

Velvet, corduroy or towelling make an effective beach mat.

This bucket is made from foam. I drew some suntan cream, added a corrugated lid and stuck it on.

Stick or stitch fabric pieces together for a beach bag with tiny string handles.

SUN CREAM
SPF 12

CROWNING

CROWN YOURSELF KING OR QUEEN FOR THE DAY! BE IT FOR A FANCY DRESS PARTY, A SCHOOL PLAY OR JUST FOR FUN! FOLLOW THE EASY STEPS FOR A VERY ROYAL ART ATTACK!

Measure around your head. If you haven't got a tape measure use a piece of string.

Cut a rectangle of card long enough to go around your head and as wide as you want your crown to be. (About 9cm for a small one and 15cm for a large one.) Cut a zig zag edge.

Join the two short ends with sticky tape. Tape twists of newspaper all around the bottom edge, then cover the crown with 3 layers of torn newspaper pasted on with diluted PVA glue.

GLORY!

When dry, paint it. Paint the whole thing white first and then paint it yellow. Paint the 'fur' trim white. Add jewels by sticking on with plenty of PVA glue. Shiny buttons could be used instead.

To make your crown really authentic, glue some white fake fur or cottonwool around the brim. Stick jewels or sequins on for royal glamour!

99

Funny Faces!

Draw your own funny faces or stick on some photos of your family members or friends. Colour to complete!

USING ACRYLICS

YOU CAN BUY ACRYLIC PAINTS FROM ANY CRAFT OR ART SHOP. THEY COME IN LOADS OF FANTASTIC COLOURS WHICH YOU CAN USE ALONE OR MIXED TOGETHER. THEY ARE EVEN WATERPROOF WHEN DRY!

TEXTURED PICTURES!

Use the paint straight from the tube to give your picture a thick textured look! Leave it to dry before adding highlights over the top. Unlike watercolour and poster paints, you can add further layers of colour over the top of previous ones.

WATERCOLOUR EFFECTS!

You can use acrylic paints like watercolours by adding small amounts of water. If you want to add highlights, you will need to leave space for them as you would when using ordinary watercolour paints.

PAPIER MACHE MAKES!

Use them to decorate papier maché models! The thick consistency of the paint means that they cover papier maché with ease.

CHUNKY C

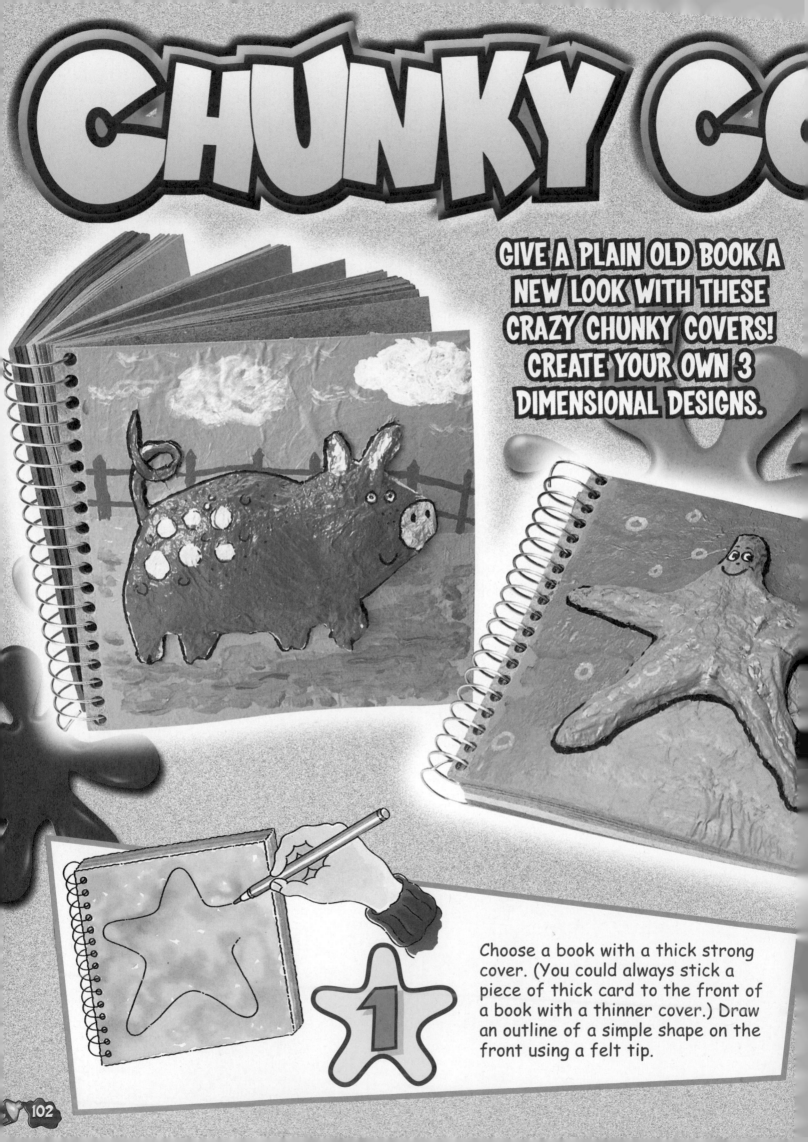

GIVE A PLAIN OLD BOOK A NEW LOOK WITH THESE CRAZY CHUNKY COVERS! CREATE YOUR OWN 3 DIMENSIONAL DESIGNS.

1

Choose a book with a thick strong cover. (You could always stick a piece of thick card to the front of a book with a thinner cover.) Draw an outline of a simple shape on the front using a felt tip.

VERS!

2 Mix 2 parts PVA glue with 1 part water. Scrunch up small bits of kitchen roll, dip in the glue mixture and stick onto the book cover, filling in the shape you have drawn. Smooth over with your finger tips.

3 Leave to dry until rock hard. Then paint with bright colours. When the paint is dry, add any details with black marker pen. When that's dry, 'varnish' by painting it with a coat of diluted PVA glue.

HOT TIPS!

Wait until the cover is dry, then outline everything with black marker pen - it will make it stand out!

Keep your designs simple, they will be more effective.

Personalise diaries, address books and photo albums with your chunky cover designs! But don't use a library or a school book!

Be careful not to soak the cover when you are using the wet kitchen roll. The cover will bend if it becomes too wet.

HERE'S A GREAT IDEA FOR AN ART BOOK!

Money Box

ALL YOU NEED TO MAKE THESE FANTASTIC MONEY BOXES ARE 2 BALLOONS, 2 DRINKING CHOCOLATE TINS, CARDBOARD BOX CARD, NEWSPAPER, PVA GLUE AND PAINT!

1 To make the toadstool caps, cover half of two balloons with five layers of papier maché. Stand the balloons in bowls to keep them steady. Leave to dry overnight.

2 Make a base from the side of a cardboard box. Attach the two drinking chocolate tins to the base. Cover the whole thing with two layers of papier maché.

3 Pop the balloons and trim the edges. Carefully cut a slot in the top of each one big enough to put coins through.

4 Place the trimmed caps on a piece of cardboard and draw around them. Cut them out and cut a circle from the middle of each. Attach them to the caps with sticky tape.

Mushrooms!

IF YOU DON'T WANT TO USE THEM AS MONEY BOXES, DON'T MAKE A COIN SLOT AT THE TOP. YOU CAN JUST LIFT THE MUSHROOM UP TO STORE THINGS IN!

5 Cut two strips of corrugated card slightly bigger than the drinking chocolate tins. Roll them into columns and secure. Then attach them to the mushroom caps with sticky tape.

6 Cover the two mushrooms with two layers of papier mâché. When dry, paint. Make sure everything is dry before putting them together.

CHOC-A-DOOD

1 Mould the main body shape on a balloon. Slosh diluted PVA glue (mixed half and half with water) and four to five layers of torn newspaper strips over the balloon.

2 Meanwhile, make the head. Get a long cardboard tube - longer than the balloon! Crumple a sheet of newspaper into a ball and attach it to the end of the tube, using sticky tape.

3 Cut shapes from cardboard and stick them to the newspaper ball until you have something that looks like a chicken's head. Stick on small crumpled paper balls for eyes. Cover with about 3 layers of papier maché. (Don't cover the other end of the tube.)

E DOO!

HOW ABOUT A CHICKEN THAT LAYS REAL CHOCOLATE EGGS? JUST TURN IT'S HEAD AND OUT POPS AN EGG!

YOU WILL NEED:

Long balloon, newspaper, PVA glue, sticky tape, cardboard or tape reels, string, kitchen roll, paints.

LOOK FOR SMALL CHOCOLATE EGGS AT PICK'N'MIX COUNTERS. DON'T EAT THEM ALL AT ONCE!

wax crayon

4 Attach a piece of cardboard tubing to form a 'neck.' Cover this with papier mâché. When the body is dry, pop the balloon. Cut a hole in the top and bottom of your papier mâché body, large enough for the cardboard tube. Cover half the hole at the bottom using small bits of card and sticky tape. Do the same with the tube.

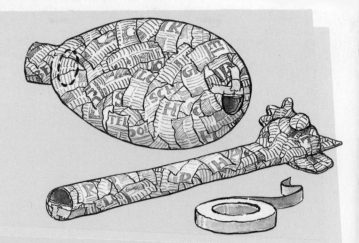

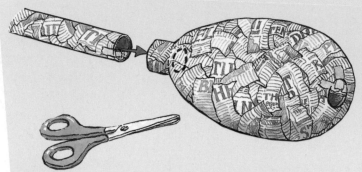

5 Now slide the tube in through the neck to see if it needs trimming. Cut any length off from the neck end.

6 Add feet! The feet are shaped like a wedge to help it stand up. Fold a strip of card measuring 200mm x 90mm in half. Tape the ends together. Block the sides off with triangles of card attached with sticky tape.

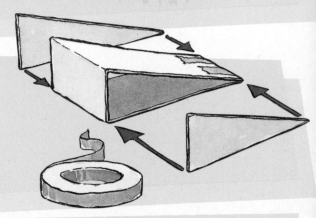

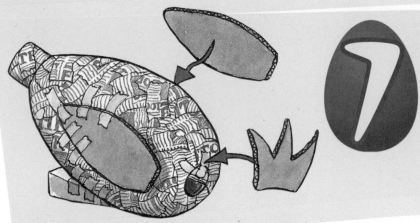

7 Add wings and a tail cut from thick cardboard. Attach them with sticky tape. Make sure the tail goes above the hole.

8 Now paint your chicken! When the paint is dry you can fill the neck with small chocolate eggs. Insert the tube into the body. Turn the head and the chicken will lay chocolate eggs!

HINTS & TIPS!

"I find it hard to cut thick cardboard..."
DAMPEN THE CARD SLIGHTLY WITH WATER - THIS WILL MAKE IT SOFTER.

"It's hard to tell when I'm starting a second layer of papier maché..."
USE ONE LAYER OF NEWSPAPER AND ONE LAYER OF MAGAZINE PAPER - YOU'LL BE ABLE TO SEE WHEN YOU'RE STARTING THE NEXT LAYER.

"My papier maché is taking ages to dry..."
TRY PUTTING IT SOMEWHERE WARM AND DRY- HOW ABOUT THE AIRING CUPBOARD?

"My papier maché isn't strong enough..."
COVER THE MODEL WITH MORE NEWSPAPER LAYERS AND LEAVE TO DRY FOR LONGER IN BETWEEN EACH LAYER.

"I haven't got strong enough cardboard..."
STICK SEVERAL PIECES OF CARD TOGETHER.

"Poster paint doesn't cover papier maché models that well..."
MIX THE PAINT WITH SOME PVA GLUE.

"It's hard moulding newspaper into small features..."
USE PULP FROM KITCHEN ROLL SOAKED IN DILUTED PVA GLUE INSTEAD.

"The paint seems to chip off my model..."
COVER YOUR PAINTED MODEL WITH A THICK LAYER OF PVA GLUE. IT WILL GO ON WHITE BUT DRY TRANSPARENT.

"I don't have any PVA glue"
MIX FLOUR AND WATER TOGETHER TO MAKE A THICK PASTE. MAKE SURE YOU GET PERMISSION FROM AN ADULT FIRST.

"I find it hard to papier maché a balloon..."
SUPPORT THE BALLOON IN A BOWL. COVER ONE HALF WITH PAPER, LEAVE IT TO DRY AND THEN TURN THE BALLOON OVER AND DO THE OTHER HALF.

ATTACK